ABT

Team Spirit

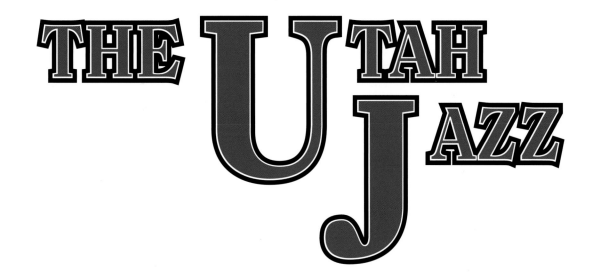

THE UTAH JAZZ

BY

MARK STEWART

Content Consultant
Matt Zeysing
Historian and Archivist
The Naismith Memorial Basketball Hall of Fame

NORWOOD HOUSE PRESS
CHICAGO, ILLINOIS

Norwood House Press
P.O. Box 316598
Chicago, Illinois 60631

For information regarding Norwood House Press, please visit our website at:
www.norwoodhousepress.com or call 866-565-2900.

All photos courtesy of AP Images—AP/Wide World Photos, Inc. except the following:
Larry Berman/BermanSports.com (6);
Topps, Inc. (14, 20, 21 bottom, 23 top, 30, 34 both, 35 top left, 40 top and bottom left, 43);
Author's Collection (35 bottom, 37).
Special thanks to Topps, Inc.

Editor: Mike Kennedy
Associate Editor: Brian Fitzgerald
Designer: Ron Jaffe
Project Management: Black Book Partners, LLC.
Special thanks to Gerald Sommer

Library of Congress Cataloging-in-Publication Data

Stewart, Mark, 1960-
   The Utah Jazz / by Mark Stewart ; content consultant, Matt
Zeysing.
      p. cm. -- (Team spirit)
   Summary: "Presents the history, accomplishments and key person-
alities of the Utah Jazz basketball team. Includes timelines, quotes,
maps, glossary and websites"--Provided by publisher.
   Includes bibliographical references and index.
   ISBN-13: 978-1-59953-127-4 (library edition : alk. paper)
   ISBN-10: 1-59953-127-5 (library edition : alk. paper)
   1. Utah Jazz (Basketball team)--History--Juvenile literature. I.
Zeysing, Matt. II. Title.
GV885.52.U8S84 2008
796.323'6409792258--dc22

                                                        2007014887

Manufactured in the United States of America.

COVER PHOTO: DeShawn Stevenson, Greg Ostertag, and Andrei Kirilenko soar
high for a rebound during a game during the 2003–04 season.

Table of Contents

SPORTS WORDS & VOCABULARY WORDS: In this book, you will find many words that are new to you. You may also see familiar words used in new ways. The glossary on page 46 gives the meanings of basketball words, as well as "everyday" words that have special basketball meanings. These words appear in **bold type** throughout the book. The glossary on page 47 gives the meanings of vocabulary words that are not related to basketball. They appear in ***bold italic type*** throughout the book.

BASKETBALL SEASONS: Because each basketball season begins late in one year and ends early in the next, seasons are not named after years. Instead, they are written out as two years separated by a dash, for example 1944–45 or 2005–06.

Meet the Jazz

Fans of jazz music love the way performers work together and mix their individual skills. Fans of basketball expect nothing less of the teams they cheer for. It takes creative and talented players to form a winning combination in the **National Basketball Association (NBA)**.

The Utah Jazz are a good example of what makes the NBA special. The team combines the talents of many different players, always finding a way to play entertaining and winning basketball. Although Utah is not known for its jazz, its basketball team could not have a better name.

This book tells the story of the Jazz. Like the music it is named after, the team began in New Orleans, Louisiana. However, it was not until they moved 2,000 miles to Utah that the Jazz learned how to *compose* a winning tune. Since then, the sound of a bouncing basketball has been sweet music to the ears of their loud and loyal fans.

Deron Williams high-fives Mehmet Okur after the Jazz score a basket.

Way Back When

The story of the Jazz begins in the city of New Orleans. Thanks to players such as Bob Pettit and Pete Maravich, college basketball became very popular in Louisiana during the 1950s and 1960s. Fans soon wanted to see **professional** basketball come to the state. In 1967, the **American Basketball Association (ABA)** put a team named the Buccaneers in New Orleans. They came within one victory of winning the championship that season.

Two years later, the Buccaneers moved up the Mississippi River to Memphis, Tennessee. Professional basketball was not finished in New Orleans, however. In 1974, the NBA placed a team there and called it the Jazz, after the world-famous music that was born in the city.

The Jazz tried to win the fans over by trading for Maravich. The deal cost them six future **draft picks**. Although "Pistol Pete" was a star, New Orleans lacked good young players who could help him turn the team around. The Jazz lost a lot of games over the next five seasons. When Maravich injured his knee and began missing time, the fans stopped coming to the team's games.

The owners of the Jazz decided to look for a new home. They chose Salt Lake City, Utah. Many years earlier, the state had hosted a very good ABA team, the Stars. Fans in Utah were excited to hear they were getting a new pro team. They supported the Jazz as they rebuilt their club, and soon Utah had an excellent team. Their top player was Adrian Dantley, who led the NBA in scoring twice.

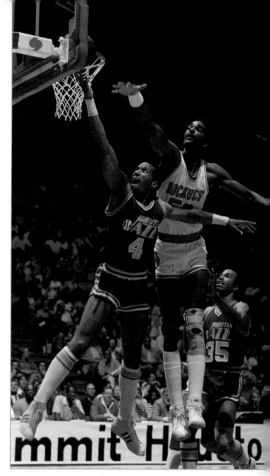

The Jazz added a number of *dynamic* players to their team in the 1980s. Mark Eaton was a mountain of a man who played defense as well as any center in the NBA. Darrell Griffith was nicknamed "Dr. Dunkenstein" for his monster jams. John Stockton saw plays unfold before anyone else on the court. This made him an excellent passer and defender. The man whose job it was to blend these talents was Utah's coach, Frank Layden. He was clever, good-natured, and loved by the players and fans.

The final piece of the puzzle for the Jazz fell into place in 1985. That year, the team **drafted** Karl Malone, a powerful forward who

LEFT: Pete Maravich takes a long shot against the New York Knicks.
ABOVE: Adrian Dantley scores against the Houston Rockets.

could run, pass, dribble, and shoot. He and Stockton became great friends, and the pair soon began thinking and playing as one. Malone would set a **pick** for Stockton and then roll toward the basket for a pass before opponents could react. Everyone who faced the Jazz knew this "pick and roll" play was coming, but no one ever figured out how to stop it.

In 1988, Jerry Sloan took over as the team's coach. He led the Jazz to the **playoffs** 15 years in a row. In 1996–97 and again in 1997–98, Utah reached the **NBA Finals**. By that time, Stockton and Malone were supported by a group of good **role players**, including Jeff Hornacek, Bryon Russell, Greg Ostertag, Shandon Anderson, Howard Eisley, and Antoine Carr.

Both times, the Jazz faced the Chicago Bulls for the NBA Championship. Each series featured close, exciting games, but the Jazz did not win either one. When Stockton and Malone left the Jazz after the 2002–03 season, the team started a new search for its first NBA title.

LEFT: John Stockton goes up for a layup. He led the Jazz for 19 seasons.
ABOVE: Karl Malone, the top scorer and rebounder in team history.

The Team Today

The Jazz learned important lessons about teamwork from John Stockton and Karl Malone. They also learned that it takes everyone on the **roster** to win a championship. In the years since those two stars retired, Utah has tried to find players with special skills and good personalities. They also search for talent in places that other NBA teams sometimes *overlook*.

The results have been remarkable. By combining American players such as Carlos Boozer, Deron Williams, and Matt Harpring with *international* stars such as Andrei Kirilenko and Mehmet Okur, Utah rebuilt quickly. Today, the Jazz have one of the league's best teams. They proved that in 2006–07 by reaching the **Western Conference Finals** for the third time in club history.

The Jazz believe that they have an excellent chance to return to the NBA Finals. The team plays with great *intensity* all the time and understands that defense is the key to winning championships. No one tries harder, gives more effort in their quest for victory, or is more involved in their community than the Jazz.

Deron Williams, Carlos Boozer, and Andrei Kirilenko play the good team defense that has made the Jazz one of the NBA's best clubs.

Home Court

For most of their time in New Orleans, the Jazz played in the Louisiana Superdome. It was the largest domed sports arena in the world when it opened. When the team moved to Utah, it played its home games in the Salt Palace, a building that had originally been the home of the Utah Stars of the ABA. It was torn down in the 1990s to make room for a **convention center**.

In 1991, the Jazz moved into the Delta Center, which was named after Delta Air Lines. While most arenas normally take up to three years to build, this project was completed in just over 15 months. All of the arena's designers, suppliers, and workers **cooperated** every day to make this happen. In 2006, the arena was renamed after a company called EnergySolutions.

BY THE NUMBERS

- *There are 19,911 seats for basketball in the Jazz's arena.*
- *The arena has 56 luxury suites.*
- *In 1991, the cost of building the team's new home was $93 million.*
- *In 2002, the Olympic figure skating competition was held in the Jazz's arena.*

Utah's arena is rocking during the 1996–97 NBA Finals.

Dressed for Success

The Jazz got their start in New Orleans, where jazz music was born. In fact, the team designed its original uniform and *logo* with a musical theme in mind.

During their years in New Orleans, the Jazz wore purple, white, and yellow uniforms. The team's logo featured a large musical note that formed the letter J. After moving west in 1979, the Jazz continued to use this logo but changed their main uniform color to green.

The Jazz later switched back to their old purple uniforms and wore them until 1996. That year, the team unveiled a stunning

LOUIE NELSON • G

new design. The musical note disappeared, and pictures of the snow-capped Utah mountains were added. The Jazz wore white at home and blue on the road. The team also created a plain, black uniform that it sometimes wore during road games. The team's current uniform reads UTAH or JAZZ across the front.

Louie Nelson models the uniform of the New Orleans Jazz.

UNIFORM BASICS

The basketball uniform is very simple. It consists of a roomy top and baggy shorts.

- The top hangs from the shoulders, with big "scoops" for the arms and neck. This style has not changed much over the years.

- Shorts, however, have changed a lot. They used to be very short, so players could move their legs freely. In the last 20 years, shorts have gotten longer and much baggier.

Basketball uniforms look the same as they did long ago … until you look very closely. In the old days, the shorts had belts and buckles. The tops were made of a thick cotton called "jersey," which got very heavy when players sweated. Later, uniforms were made of shiny **satin**. They may have looked great, but they did not "breathe." As a result, players got very hot! Today, most uniforms are made of **synthetic** materials that soak up sweat and keep the body cool.

Carlos Boozer takes a shot in the team's 2006–07 blue road uniform.

We Won!

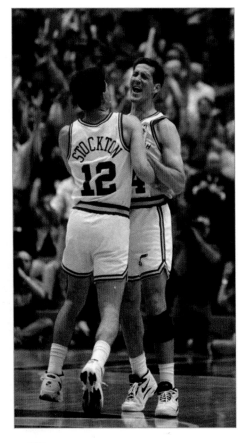

The Jazz have played in the NBA's **Western Conference** since they moved to Utah in 1979. The conference is known for its quick, exciting players and its fast-paced basketball. The Jazz usually did very well against their Western Conference opponents during the regular season. However, when the playoffs began, they often found themselves *overmatched*. Time and again, the Jazz's hopes of reaching the NBA Finals were crushed by teams that they had beaten earlier in the year.

For many years, Utah fans believed that the team needed to add a great center. Jerry Sloan did not agree. The Utah coach thought that John Stockton and Karl Malone were like two points on a triangle. To be successful, he said, the team needed a third point to *complement* them. Sloan found that player during the 1993–94 season when the Jazz traded for Jeff Hornacek. He was a hardworking guard who kept his cool during close games. When opponents **double-teamed** Stockton or crowded around Malone, Hornacek was usually wide open. He calmly made **3-pointers** as if he were shooting in his driveway.

By 1996–97, the Jazz were unstoppable. They won 64 games and finished first in their **division**. In the playoffs, Utah easily defeated the Los Angeles Clippers and the Los Angeles Lakers in the first two rounds. All that stood between the Jazz and their first Western Conference championship were the Houston Rockets.

Houston was a *formidable* opponent with three Hall of Fame players—Hakeem Olajuwon, Charles Barkley, and Clyde Drexler. The Jazz, however, had Malone, the league's **Most Valuable Player (MVP)**. In Game 1, he led Utah to a 101–86 victory with 21 points and 13 rebounds.

The teams split the next four games, giving Utah a three games to two lead. Game 6 was played in Houston, and Rockets fans cheered wildly as their team led by seven points with two minutes to go. Just when

LEFT: John Stockton and Jeff Hornacek celebrate a Jazz victory.
ABOVE: Karl Malone scores against the Rockets.

17

the Jazz looked beaten, Bryon Russell hit a 3-point shot to make the score 98–94. Then Stockton made two layups to tie the contest. After two free throws by Barkley, Stockton tied the game again with a difficult off-balance shot.

With just a few seconds left, Utah got the ball back. Malone set a **screen** for Stockton, who received a pass and fired a shot from 25 feet away as the buzzer sounded. The ball swished for a 103–100 win. The Jazz were conference champs!

One year later, Utah returned to the Western Conference Finals. This time they played Shaquille O'Neal, Kobe Bryant, and the Lakers. The Jazz desperately wanted another shot at the NBA Championship. It showed in Game 1, when they destroyed Los Angeles 112–77. It was the worst loss in the Lakers' history.

The Jazz kept pouring it on after that. They won the next three in a row to take the series in four games. Utah proved that when teammates help each other on defense and share the ball on offense, even the mighty Lakers can be swept off the court.

Malone was the hero in Game 4 with 32 points. "I think the whole nation is surprised by the sweep," he said. "We just took it one game at a time and had the killer instinct."

Kobe Bryant and Elden Campbell can only watch as Bryon Russell dunks against the Lakers.

Go-To Guys

To be a true star in the NBA, you need more than a great shot. You have to be a "go-to guy"—someone teammates trust to make the winning play when the seconds are ticking away in a big game. Jazz fans have had a lot to cheer about over the years, including these great stars …

THE PIONEERS

PETE MARAVICH   6' 5" Guard

- BORN: 6/22/1947   • DIED: 1/5/1988
- PLAYED FOR TEAM: 1974–75 TO 1979–80

Pete Maravich was the NBA's best dribbler, passer, and shooter when he played for the Jazz. He made one amazing basket after another, yet he rarely let a smile cross his lips. "Pistol Pete" had a deep desire to score—and a deeper desire to win.

ADRIAN DANTLEY   6' 5" Guard/Forward

- BORN: 2/28/1955   • PLAYED FOR TEAM: 1979–80 TO 1985–86

No one ever figured out how to play defense against Adrian Dantley. He was too quick for forwards and too big for guards. Dantley led the NBA in scoring in 1980–81 and 1983–84. He was also among Utah's leaders in rebounds and **assists** every year.

ABOVE: Pete Maravich
TOP RIGHT: Darrell Griffith   **BOTTOM RIGHT**: Thurl Bailey

DARRELL GRIFFITH　　　　　6' 4" Guard

- Born: 6/16/1958
- Played for Team: 1980–81 to 1990–91

When Utah's opponents lost track of Darrell Griffith, they paid a steep price. He was a great leaper who soared through the air and slammed the ball through the basket. Griffith averaged 20 points a game in 1983–84, the first year the Jazz made the playoffs.

MARK EATON　　　　　7' 4" Center

- Born: 1/24/1957
- Played for Team: 1982–83 to 1992–93

Mark Eaton's college coaches thought he was too big and clumsy to be a starting player. In the NBA, he proved them wrong. In 1984–85, Eaton set a record for blocked shots in a season. He was named Defensive Player of the Year twice.

THURL BAILEY　　　　　6' 11" Forward

- Born: 4/7/1961
- Played for Team: 1983–84 to 1991–92 & 1998–99

Thurl Bailey had the ability to "read" a game and know instantly what he needed to do on the court. Some nights he scored, and some nights he kept the other team's star from scoring. Most nights he did a little of everything. Bailey loved Utah and became very close to the state and its fans.

MODERN STARS

JOHN STOCKTON   6' 1"   Guard

• BORN: 3/26/1962   • PLAYED FOR TEAM: 1984–85 TO 2002–03

When John Stockton had the ball in his hands, he was an artist and the court was his canvas. He often knew when his teammates would be open before they did, and his smart passes set them up for easy shots. Stockton led the NBA in assists nine times and had 15,806 assists for his career—over 5,000 more than anyone else in history.

KARL MALONE   6' 9"   Forward

• BORN: 7/24/1963   • PLAYED FOR TEAM: 1985–86 TO 2002–03

Karl Malone combined tremendous strength and *agility* to become the greatest **power forward** of his era. There were many times when he was almost impossible to stop. Most teams decided the best *strategy* was to foul Malone. They were wrong. He shot—and made—more free throws than any player in history.

JEFF HORNACEK   6' 3"   Guard

• BORN: 5/3/1963

• PLAYED FOR TEAM: 1993–94 TO 1999-2000

Jeff Hornacek was a tough player with an accurate 3-point shot. With Malone keeping defenders busy inside, Hornacek was often wide open for shots from outside. His **clutch** scoring and *hard-nosed* defense helped make the Jazz an extremely difficult team to beat.

ABOVE: Jeff Hornacek   **TOP RIGHT**: Andrei Kirilenko
BOTTOM RIGHT: NBA Commissioner David Stern congratulates Deron Williams on draft day.

ANDREI KIRILENKO   6' 8"   **Forward**

- BORN: 2/18/1981
- FIRST SEASON WITH TEAM: 2001–02

The Jazz drafted Andrei Kirilenko when he was a teenager and patiently waited for him to join the team. When he arrived in Utah, Kirilenko amazed everyone with his ability to block shots and steal passes. He soon became a good scorer, too.

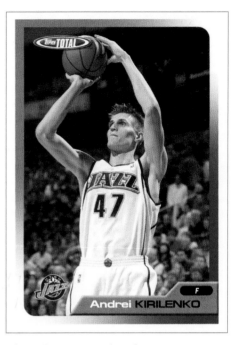

MEHMET OKUR   6' 11"   **Center**

- BORN: 5/26/1979
- FIRST SEASON WITH TEAM: 2004–05

As a role player with the Detroit Pistons, Mehmet Okur became the first Turkish player to win an NBA Championship. With the Jazz, he was able to put his full game on display. Okur quickly showed that he was one of the best-shooting centers in the league.

DERON WILLIAMS   6' 3"   **Guard**

- BORN: 6/26/1984
- FIRST SEASON WITH TEAM: 2005–06

The Jazz were delighted when they were able to draft Deron Williams in 2005. Williams was a tough guard who proved he could handle a lot of responsibility when he led his college team to within one victory of the **National Championship**. He continued to shine in the NBA.

On the Sidelines

When the Jazz played in New Orleans, they had trouble finding the right people to run the team. Their first president made trades that crippled the club. Their first coach was fired after just a few games. Things finally began to change in 1979, when the Jazz hired Frank Layden to handle the team's business. They soon realized that he would make a good coach, too.

During the 1980s, Layden turned the Jazz into a winning team. He was a smart coach, a superb teacher, and one of basketball's all-time great *characters*. Layden encouraged his players to work together. He found *imaginative* ways to combine their skills, which made the Jazz a hard team to beat.

When poor health forced Layden to retire from coaching, he chose Jerry Sloan to follow him. Sloan was known as a hard worker during his playing days. He showed the Jazz that a little extra effort often meant the difference between victory and defeat. Sloan led Utah to the NBA Finals twice and won his 1,000th game as coach of the Jazz in 2007.

Jerry Sloan shouts instructions to the Jazz from the Utah sideline.

One Great Day

When the 1993 NBA **All-Star Game** began in Salt Lake City, all anyone wanted to talk about was how many exciting young players were in uniform. By the final buzzer, however, the biggest cheers were saved for a couple of "old-timers"—John Stockton and Karl Malone.

All-Star Games can be boring. The players are not used to each other, and they play more slowly and carefully than usual. This game was different. Stockton attacked the East's defense and made great passes to his West teammates, including Malone, David Robinson, and Charles Barkley. The East, led by Michael Jordan, competed just as hard.

The teams might have started the game playing for fun, but soon the contest became a battle for pride. Whenever the West needed a basket, Paul Westphal—the coach of the team—would call proven plays for Stockton and Malone. Even against All-Star competition, the duo was impossible to stop.

The game was close from start to finish. The lead changed hands 17 times. At the end of 48 minutes, the score was tied 119–119. The teams played a thrilling five-minute **overtime**. Barkley and Dan Majerle made 3-pointers to put the West ahead. When the East tried to fight back, Stockton and Malone took over. Stockton scored two baskets and dished out two assists, and Malone made a jump shot that sealed the victory. The West won 135–132.

When it came time to pick the game's MVP, the voters could not decide between Malone and Stockton. Malone had 28 points and 10 rebounds. Stockton recorded 15 assists, seven to his Jazz teammate. When the decision was announced, the crowd roared its approval. The two Utah stars were named co-MVPs.

"If you wrote a movie," Malone smiled in the locker room, "that's how it would end."

LEFT: Karl Malone blocks a shot by Charles Barkley. These fierce rivals were teammates during the 1993 All-Star Game.   **ABOVE**: Stockton and Malone show off their MVP trophy to the hometown fans in Utah.

Legend Has It

When did Karl Malone get his famous nickname?

LEGEND HAS IT that he was first called the "Mailman" during his college days. Malone attended Louisiana Tech University. The students there admired his hard work in the classroom and on the basketball court. Game after game, he showed up and gave the Bulldogs points, rebounds, and good defense. Fans nicknamed Malone the "Mailman" because he could be counted upon to deliver again and again.

ABOVE: Karl Malone, also known as the "Mailman."
RIGHT: Mark Eaton covers Kareem Abdul-Jabbar.

Which Jazz player has a famous basketball father-in-law?

LEGEND HAS IT that Andrei Kirilenko does. His wife, Masha, is the daughter of Andrei Lapatov, who played for the Soviet Union's basketball team during the 1980s. In all, Lapatov was an international basketball star for 14 years.

Which Jazz player was once a water polo star?

LEGEND HAS IT that Mark Eaton was. Eaton loved being in the water as a child. As he grew taller and heavier, he was encouraged to compete on the basketball court. Eaton, however, felt more graceful—and less *self-conscious*—in the pool. He went on to star on his high school's water polo team. After graduation, Eaton became an auto mechanic and did not play basketball seriously until he was in his 20s.

It Really Happened

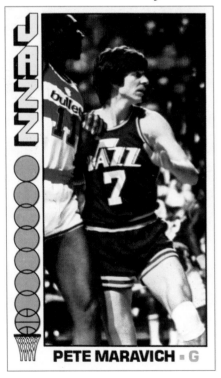

PETE MARAVICH • G

Pete Maravich loved an audience. The more people watching, the better Maravich played. "If there is one thing that really turns me on, it's playing in front of a lot of people," he once admitted.

On February 25th, 1977, Maravich was right where he wanted to be. The Jazz faced the New York Knicks in the Louisiana Superdome. There were more than 11,000 fans in the stands, which was a big crowd for New Orleans. Back in New York, hundreds of thousands of Knicks fans were glued to their television sets.

Some of the best players in the NBA were on the court that night, including Walt Frazier. A seven-time member of the league's **All-Defensive team**, he was guarding Maravich. The game was barely a few minutes old when the crowd started to sense that something special was happening. No matter what Frazier did, he could not keep "Pistol Pete" from scoring.

Maravich scored 13 of his team's first 19 points. He was making shots from 25 feet, and he was scoring on twisting **drives** to the basket. At halftime, the Jazz led 65–43, and Maravich had 31 points.

In the second half, New York put young Ticky Burden on Maravich. Pistol Pete launched three long bombs and they all went in. With nine minutes left in the game, Maravich had already broken his own personal record of 51 points.

The baskets kept coming. More long jump shots and a reverse layup brought the crowd to its feet. Maravich could not miss. Even *he* had to smile when he spun a bank shot into the net with his back to the basket.

With two minutes left, Maravich stole a pass and went the length of the court for an easy layup. That gave him 68 points. Moments later, Maravich was called for an **offensive foul**. It was his sixth of the game, which meant he had to take a seat on the bench. The Jazz went on to win 124–107, and Maravich had the single-game scoring record for NBA guards.

LEFT: Pete Maravich is shown playing defense on this 1977 trading card.
ABOVE: Maravich makes a move to the basket.

Team Spirit

Salt Lake City is nestled in the Rocky Mountains, so there are many fun sports and activities that compete with basketball. Many of the people who root for the Jazz are athletes themselves. They love extreme sports such as snowboarding, rock climbing, mountain biking, and kayaking. Still, a good seat at a Jazz game is like a golden ticket.

No athlete in Utah is more extreme than Jazz Bear, the team's mascot. He will try anything on a bike, stilts, or skates. If it is weird and thrills the crowd, Jazz Bear will do it! Utah fans are also entertained by the Jazz Dancers and the Jazz Stunt Team.

The Jazz and their players reach out to their fans all year long. The team's Jr. Jazz basketball fundamentals program takes place in Utah and five surrounding states. More than 60,000 kids participate in Jr. Jazz, which makes it one of the largest youth sports organizations in the world.

All eyes are on Jazz Bear as he grabs some air during his halftime show.

Timeline

The basketball season is played from October through June. That means each season takes place at the end of one year and halfway through the next. In this timeline, the accomplishments of the Jazz are shown by season.

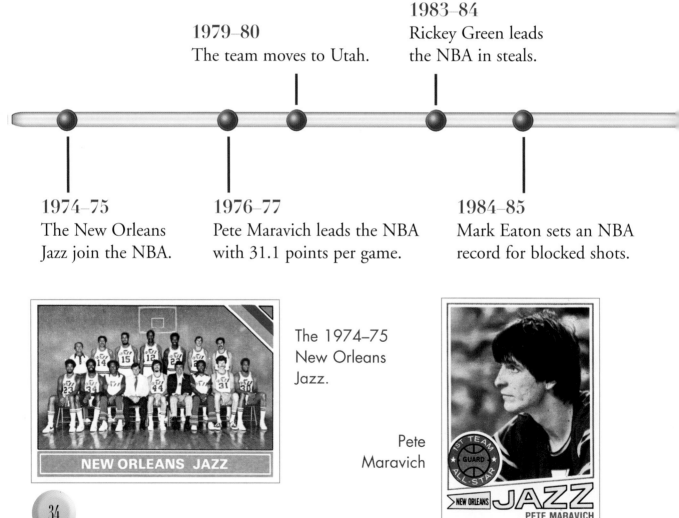

1979–80
The team moves to Utah.

1983–84
Rickey Green leads the NBA in steals.

1974–75
The New Orleans Jazz join the NBA.

1976–77
Pete Maravich leads the NBA with 31.1 points per game.

1984–85
Mark Eaton sets an NBA record for blocked shots.

NEW ORLEANS JAZZ

The 1974–75 New Orleans Jazz.

Pete Maravich

NEW ORLEANS JAZZ
PETE MARAVICH

John
Stockton

Andrei Kirilenko
blocks a shot.

1992–93
John Stockton and Karl Malone are
co-MVPs of the All-Star Game.

2005–06
Andrei Kirilenko is named to
the NBA All-Defensive Team.

1996–97
The Jazz reach the
NBA Finals for the
first time.

1998–99
Malone wins his
second MVP award.

2002–03
Malone and Stockton play
their final seasons for the team.

A souvenir
pennant from
the team's first
trip to the
NBA Finals.

Fun Facts

NICE GUYS FINISH FIRST

In 1984, Frank Layden won the J. Walter Kennedy Citizenship Award. It is given each year to the person who does the most for the basketball community. Layden was the first coach in history to receive the award.

KEEP ON TRUCKIN' BABY!

Karl Malone had one of the NBA's most unusual hobbies. Between seasons, he hauled cargo in his 18-wheel truck.

TOUGH TO BEAT

When John Stockton retired in 2003, he held three records that may never be broken. He was the NBA's all-time leader in assists (15,806), steals (3,265), and seasons played for the same team (19).

ABOVE: Frank Layden
RIGHT: The cover of a New Orleans yearbook features Pete Maravich and Truck Robinson, the team's top players in the 1970s.

INTERNATIONAL TRADE

In 1988, the Jazz traded Mel Turpin to a pro team in Spain for Jose Ortiz. Both players had to approve the deal. It was the first time in history an NBA player was traded to another country.

YOUNG GUN

Pete Maravich was elected to the **Basketball Hall of Fame** at the age of 39. He was the youngest person ever to receive this honor.

CHAIRMAN OF THE BOARDS

In 1977–78, Leonard "Truck" Robinson led the NBA with 15.8 rebounds per game. He was the first rebounding champion in Jazz history. Robinson had 27 rebounds in a game twice that season.

ON A DIFFERENT NOTE

During his years with the Jazz, Thurl Bailey was known as a man of many talents. A few years after he retired, he recorded a CD called *Faith In Your Heart*, which won several awards.

Talking Hoops

"I want to do something good, especially in crunch time."
—*Andrei Kirilenko, on saving his best for when the team needs it most*

"They traded three first-round draft picks to get me, so they are expecting a lot."
—*Deron Williams, on the pressure of being a young leader*

"I'm coaching almost the same team that I played for."
—*Jerry Sloan, on his hard-nosed Jazz teams of the 1990s and his rough-and-tough Chicago Bulls of the 1970s*

"I always played as hard as I could to be successful. The hard work paid off."
—*Jeff Hornacek, on how he became an All-Star*

ABOVE: Jerry Sloan
RIGHT: John Stockton and Karl Malone

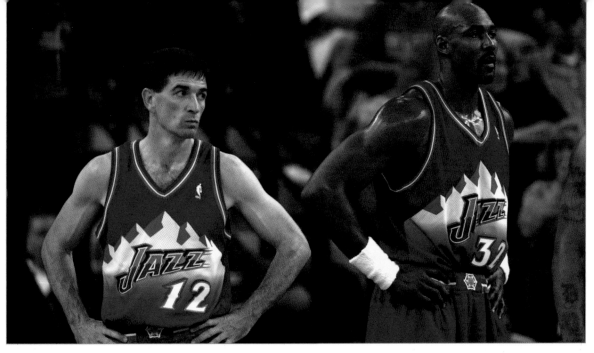

"There's so much talk about being in 'the zone' with a jumper, but you can get in a similar 'zone' as a **playmaker**."

—*John Stockton, on what made him a great point guard*

"Just because I'm a professional basketball player, don't tell me I've got to get out of a limo, I've got to wear gold chains … I'm not like that."

—*Karl Malone, on not being phony*

"They don't pay you a million dollars for two-hand chest passes."

—*Pete Maravich, on why he added extra flair to his shooting, dribbling, and passing*

"You have to make life fun."

—*Frank Layden, on his approach to coaching*

For the Record

The great Jazz teams and players have left their marks on the record books. These are the "best of the best"…

Mark Eaton

Karl Malone

JAZZ AWARD WINNERS

WINNER	AWARD	SEASON
Darrell Griffith	NBA Rookie of the Year*	1980–81
Frank Layden	NBA Coach of the Year	1983–84
Mark Eaton	NBA Defensive Player of the Year	1984–85
Karl Malone	NBA All-Star Game MVP	1988–89
Mark Eaton	NBA Defensive Player of the Year	1988–89
Karl Malone	NBA All-Star Game co-MVP	1992–93
John Stockton	NBA All-Star Game co-MVP	1992–93
Karl Malone	NBA Most Valuable Player	1996–97
Jeff Hornacek	NBA 3-Point Shootout Champion	1997–98
Karl Malone	NBA Most Valuable Player	1998–99
Jeff Hornacek	NBA 3-Point Shootout Champion	1999–00

The Rookie of the Year award is given to the league's best first-year player.

Jeff Malone, a member of the 1991–92 division champions.

JAZZ ACHIEVEMENTS

ACHIEVEMENT	SEASON
Midwest Division Champions	1983–84
Midwest Division Champions	1988–89
Midwest Division Champions	1991–92
Midwest Division Champions	1996–97
Western Conference Champions	1996–97
Midwest Division Champions	1997–98
Western Conference Champions	1997–98
Midwest Division Champions*	1998–99
Midwest Division Champions	1999–00

Tied for first place

ABOVE: Darrell Griffith, the 1980–81 Rookie of the Year.
LEFT: Greg Ostertag and Karl Malone, the big men who led the Jazz to the NBA Finals.

Pinpoints

The history of a basketball team is made up of many smaller stories. These stories take place all over the map—not just in the city a team calls "home." Match the pushpins on these maps to the Team Facts and you will begin to see the story of the Jazz unfold!

TEAM FACTS

1 Salt Lake City, Utah—*The Jazz have played here since 1979.*

2 Spokane, Washington—*John Stockton was born here.*

3 Westminster, California—*Mark Eaton was born here.*

4 McLeansboro, Illinois—*Jerry Sloan was born here.*

5 Louisville, Kentucky—*Darrell Griffith was born here.*

6 Aliquippa, Pennsylvania—*Pete Maravich was born here.*

7 Washington, D.C.—*Adrian Dantley was born here.*

8 Mobile, Alabama—*Jeff Malone was born here.*

9 New Orleans, Louisiana—*The Jazz played here from 1974 to 1979.*

10 Juneau, Alaska—*Carlos Boozer was born here.*

11 Izhevsk, Russia—*Andrei Kirilenko was born here.*

12 Yalova, Turkey—*Mehmet Okur was born here.*

Mehmet Okur

43

Play Ball

Basketball is a sport played by two teams of five players. NBA games have four 12-minute quarters—48 minutes in all—and the team that scores the most points when time has run out is the winner. Most baskets count for two points. Players who make shots from beyond the 3-point line receive an extra point. Baskets made from the free-throw line count for one point. Free throws are penalty shots awarded to a team, usually after an opponent has committed a foul. A foul is called when one player makes hard contact with another.

Players can move around all they want, but the player with the ball cannot. He must bounce the ball with one hand or the other (but never both) in order to go from one part of the court to another. As long as he keeps "dribbling," he can keep moving.

In the NBA, teams must attempt a shot within 24 seconds, so there is little time to waste. The job of the defense is to make it as difficult as possible for the offense to take a good shot—and to grab the ball if the other team shoots and misses.

This may sound simple, but anyone who has played the game knows that basketball can be very complicated. Every player on the court has a job to do. Different players have different strengths and weaknesses. The coach must mix these players in just the right way and teach them to work together as one.

The more you play and watch basketball, the more "little things" you are likely to notice. The next time you watch a game, look for these plays:

PLAY LIST

ALLEY-OOP—A play in which the passer throws the ball just to the side of the rim—so a teammate can catch it and dunk in one motion.

BACK-DOOR PLAY—A play in which the passer waits for a teammate to fake the defender away from the basket—then throws him the ball when he cuts back toward the basket.

KICK-OUT—A play in which the ball handler waits for the defense to surround him—then quickly passes to a teammate who is open for an outside shot. The ball is not really kicked in this play; the term comes from the action of pinball machines.

NO-LOOK PASS—A play in which a passer fools the defense by looking in one direction, then making a surprise pass to a teammate in another direction.

PICK-AND-ROLL—A play in which one player blocks, or "picks off," a teammate's defender with his body, then in the confusion cuts to the basket for a pass.

Glossary

BASKETBALL WORDS TO KNOW

3-POINTERS—Baskets made from behind the 3-point line.

ALL-DEFENSIVE TEAM—An honor given at the end of each season to the NBA's best defensive players at each position.

ALL-STAR GAME—The annual game in which the best players from the East and the West play against each other. The game does not count in the standings.

AMERICAN BASKETBALL ASSOCIATION (ABA)—The basketball league that played for nine seasons starting in 1967. Prior to the 1976–77 season, four ABA teams joined the NBA, and the rest went out of business.

ASSISTS—Passes that lead to successful shots.

BASKETBALL HALL OF FAME—The museum in Springfield, Massachusetts where the game's greatest players are honored; these players are often called "Hall of Famers."

CLUTCH—Able to perform well under pressure.

DIVISION—A group of teams within a league that play in the same part of the country.

DOUBLE-TEAMED—Guarded by two players.

DRAFT PICKS—College players selected or "drafted" by NBA teams each summer.

DRAFTED—Selected from a group of the best college players. The NBA draft is held each summer.

DRIVES—Strong moves to the basket.

MOST VALUABLE PLAYER (MVP)—The award given each year to the league's best player; also given to the best player in the league finals and All-Star Game.

NATIONAL BASKETBALL ASSOCIATION (NBA)—The professional league that has been operating since 1946–47.

NATIONAL CHAMPIONSHIP—The title that college basketball teams play for at the end of each season.

NBA FINALS—The playoff series that decides the champion of the league.

OFFENSIVE FOUL—A foul committed by a member of the team controlling the ball.

OVERTIME—The extra period played when a game is tied after 48 minutes.

PICK—A way of helping a teammate get open by blocking his defender with the body. Similar to a screen.

PLAYMAKER—Someone who helps his teammates score by passing the ball.

PLAYOFFS—The games played after the season to determine the league champion.

POWER FORWARD—The bigger and stronger of a team's two forwards.

PROFESSIONAL—Describes a player or team that plays a sport for money. College players are not paid, so they are considered "amateurs."

ROLE PLAYERS—People who are asked to do specific things when they are in a game.

ROSTER—The list of players on a team.

SCREEN—A way of helping a teammate get open by creating an obstacle that his defender must go around. Similar to a pick.

WESTERN CONFERENCE—A group of teams that play in the West. The winner of the Western Conference meets the winner of the Eastern Conference in the league finals.

WESTERN CONFERENCE FINALS—The playoff series that determines which team from the West will play the best team in the East for the NBA Championship.

OTHER WORDS TO KNOW

AGILITY—Being quick and graceful.

CHARACTERS—Interesting or amusing people.

COMPLEMENT—Complete or enhance.

COMPOSE—Write or create.

CONVENTION CENTER—A place where large business meetings are held.

COOPERATED—Worked together as a team.

DYNAMIC—Exciting and energetic.

FORMIDABLE—Impressive or powerful.

HARD-NOSED—Able to meet opposition head-on.

IMAGINATIVE—Creative.

INTENSITY—The strength and energy of a thought or action.

INTERNATIONAL—From all over the world.

LOGO—A symbol or design that represents a company or team.

OVERLOOK—Fail to see or notice.

OVERMATCHED—Weaker or having fewer skills than an opponent.

SATIN—A smooth, shiny fabric.

SELF-CONSCIOUS—Worried about one's appearance.

STRATEGY—A plan or method for succeeding.

SYNTHETIC—Made in a laboratory, not in nature.

Places to Go

ON THE ROAD

UTAH JAZZ
301 West South Temple
Salt Lake City, Utah 84101
(801) 325-2500

**NAISMITH MEMORIAL
BASKETBALL HALL OF FAME**
1000 West Columbus Avenue
Springfield, Massachusetts 01105
(877) 4HOOPLA

ON THE WEB

THE NATIONAL BASKETBALL ASSOCIATION   www.nba.com
  • *Learn more about the league's teams, players, and history*

THE UTAH JAZZ   www.utahjazz.com
  • *Learn more about the Utah Jazz*

THE BASKETBALL HALL OF FAME   www.hoophall.com
  • *Learn more about history's greatest players*

ON THE BOOKSHELF

To learn more about the sport of basketball, look for these books at your library or bookstore:

  • Thomas, Keltie. *How Basketball Works.* Berkeley, CA: Maple Tree Press, distributed through Publishers Group West, 2005.

  • Hareas, John. *Basketball.* New York, NY: Dorling Kindersley, 2005.

  • Hughes, Morgan. *Basketball.* Vero Beach, FL: Rourke Publishing, 2005.

Index

The Team

MARK STEWART has written more than 20 books on basketball, and over 100 sports books for kids. He grew up in New York City during the 1960s rooting for the Knicks and Nets, and now takes his two daughters, Mariah and Rachel, to watch them play. Mark comes from a family of writers. His grandfather was Sunday Editor of *The New York Times* and his mother was Articles Editor of *The Ladies' Home Journal* and *McCall's*. Mark has profiled hundreds of athletes over the last 20 years. He has also written several books about his native New York, and New Jersey, his home today. Mark is a graduate of Duke University, with a degree in History. He lives with his daughters and wife Sarah overlooking Sandy Hook, New Jersey.

MATT ZEYSING is the resident historian at the Basketball Hall of Fame in Springfield, Massachusetts. His research interests include the origins of the game of basketball, the development of professional basketball in the first half of the 20th century, and the culture and meaning of basketball in American society.